The Base-lined Stress Assessment Chart that follows is an initial assessment of one's emotional personality or stress coping abilities or life scenario.

Stress is a generic term for uncomfortable living. The term Stress, in and of its "SELF" is meaningless.

The main book in The Health, Diet and Recipe's Adventure Book Series entitled: Eating For Self: You're NOT Eating For YOU, examines and removes "STRESS" from our "True Life."

To begin the journey and adventure back to "True Foods" and "True Life," for the next 7 days and/or nights, fill in the times YOU eat in the mornings, afternoons and evenings or after or before midnight and what YOU eat?

Up next, "Equational Poetry" will assess your scores and their meanings and whether or NOT you're ready for the journey?

YOU may have to visit a website?

The Equational Poetry True Foods Journal: Eating For "SELF" is MORE than a personal food journal, It's a personal guide, along the Health, Diet, and Recipe's Adventure Book Series, back to "True Foods" and "True Life."

As such, it begins with a stress assessment to determine if one is relaxed enough to begin the journey and adventure?

The stress assessment is base-lined on 7 days of data.

The scores will be assessed by "Equational Poetry" and provided later.

Side Note: The reason for Morning = Breakfast, Afternoon = Lunch, Evening = Dinner is to get YOU away from these commercial ideas.

Stop thinking in terms of Breakfast, Lunch and Dinner and remove the word Snack from your vocabulary.

I recall when Brunch was invented to fill the dead period in between "Breakfast" & "Lunch" to increase sales.

STOP doing what CORPORATISM tells YOU. That's the problem with the news and the smartphone too.

STOP splurging on occasions and giving your "SELF" permission to sin.
Holidays are all commercial events and meaningless outside the traditional "True Life" event.

Abundance, selection and variety are NOT signs of prosperity or success. They are signs that "WE" forgot "True Life."

Think in terms of morning, afternoon and evening hunger, NOT Breakfast, Lunch and Dinner. The notion of Snack is foolish.

Join The Poetries' mailing list:
https://sendfox.com/poetries

Equational Poetry

Basline Stress Assessment Chart

TRUE FOODS FOR "TRUE LIFE"

TRUE FOOD JOURNAL

Day	Time	Morning	Afternoon	Evening
1				
2				
3				
4				
5				
6				
7				
SCORES:				

Side Notes:

Date:

Mood:

Morning = Breakfast   Afternoon = Lunch   Evening = Dinner

Equational Poetry

Basline Stress Assessment Chart

TRUE FOODS FOR "TRUE LIFE"

TRUE FOOD JOURNAL

Day	Time	Morning	Afternoon	Evening
1				
2				
3				
4				
5				
6				
7				
SCORES:				

Side Notes:

Date:

Mood:

Morning = Breakfast   Afternoon = Lunch   Evening = Dinner

Equational Poetry

Basline Stress Assessment Chart

TRUE FOODS FOR "TRUE LIFE"

TRUE FOOD JOURNAL

Day	Time	Morning	Afternoon	Evening
1				
2				
3				
4				
5				
6				
7				
SCORES:				

Side Notes:

Date:

Mood:

Morning = Breakfast   Afternoon = Lunch   Evening = Dinner

Equational Poetry

Basline Stress Assessment Chart

TRUE FOODS FOR "TRUE LIFE"

TRUE FOOD JOURNAL

Day	Time	Morning	Afternoon	Evening
1				
2				
3				
4				
5				
6				
7				
SCORES:				

Side Notes:

Date:

Mood:

Morning = Breakfast   Afternoon = Lunch   Evening = Dinner

SHOT ON REDMI 7
AI DUAL CAMERA

Equational Poetry

Everyday Eating For "SELF" Chart

TRUE FOODS FOR "TRUE LIFE"

TRUE FOOD JOURNAL

Day	Time	Morning	Afternoon	Evening
1				
2				
3				
4				
5				
6				
7				

Side Notes:

Date:

Mood:

Morning = Breakfast   Afternoon = Lunch   Evening = Dinner

2

SHOT ON P[ONE 7
AI DUAL CAMERA

Equational Poetry

Everyday Eating For "SELF" Chart

TRUE FOODS FOR "TRUE LIFE"

TRUE FOOD JOURNAL

Day	Time	Morning	Afternoon	Evening
1				
2				
3				
4				
5				
6				
7				

Side Notes:

Date:

Mood:

Morning = Breakfast   Afternoon = Lunch   Evening = Dinner

Equational Poetry

Everyday Eating For "SELF" Chart

TRUE FOODS FOR "TRUE LIFE"

TRUE FOOD JOURNAL

Day	Time	Morning	Afternoon	Evening
1				
2				
3				
4				
5				
6				
7				

Side Notes:

Date:

Mood:

Morning = Breakfast   Afternoon = Lunch   Evening = Dinner

SHOT ON REDMI 7
AI DUAL CAMERA

SHOT ON REDMI 7
AI DUAL CAMERA

Equational Poetry

Everyday Eating For "SELF" Chart

TRUE FOODS FOR "TRUE LIFE"

TRUE FOOD JOURNAL

Day	Time	Morning	Afternoon	Evening
1				
2				
3				
4				
5				
6				
7				

Side Notes:

Date:

Mood:

Morning = Breakfast   **Afternoon = Lunch**   **Evening = Dinner**

SHOT ON REDMI 7
AI DUAL CAMERA

SHOT ON REDMI 7
AI DUAL CAMERA

Equational Poetry

Everyday Eating For "SELF" Chart

TRUE FOODS FOR "TRUE LIFE"

TRUE FOOD JOURNAL

Day	Time	Morning	Afternoon	Evening
1				
2				
3				
4				
5				
6				
7				

Side Notes:

Date:

Mood:

Morning = Breakfast   Afternoon = Lunch   Evening = Dinner

SHOT ON REDMI 7
AI DUAL CAMERA

Equational Poetry

Everyday Eating For "SELF" Chart

TRUE FOODS FOR "TRUE LIFE"

TRUE FOOD JOURNAL

Day	Time	Morning	Afternoon	Evening
1				
2				
3				
4				
5				
6				
7				

Side Notes:

Date:

Mood:

Morning = Breakfast   Afternoon = Lunch   Evening = Dinner

SHOT ON REDMI 7
AI DUAL CAMERA

SHOT ON REDMI 7
AI DUAL CAMERA

7

Equational Poetry

Everyday Eating For "SELF" Chart

TRUE FOODS FOR "TRUE LIFE"

TRUE FOOD JOURNAL

Day	Time	Morning	Afternoon	Evening
1				
2				
3				
4				
5				
6				
7				

Side Notes:

Date:

Mood:

Morning = Breakfast   Afternoon = Lunch   Evening = Dinner

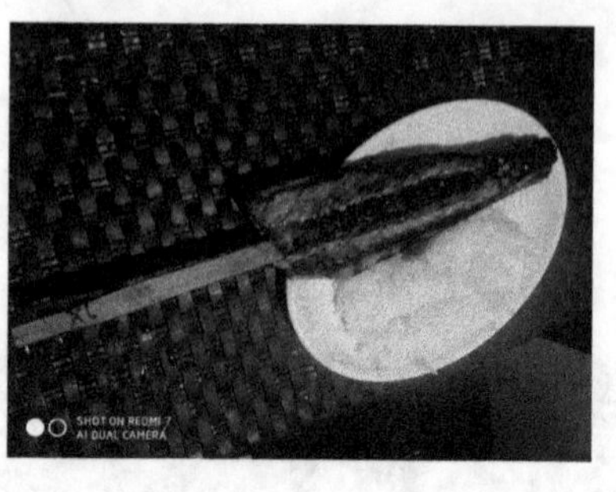

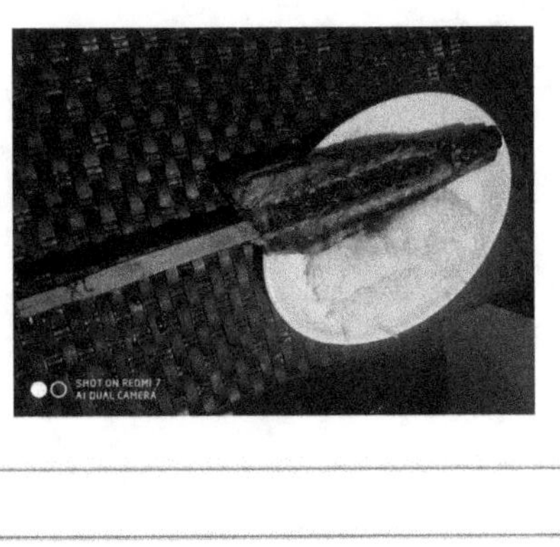

SHOT ON REDMI 7
AI DUAL CAMERA

SHOT ON REDMI 7
AI DUAL CAMERA

4

Equational Poetry

Everyday Eating For "SELF" Chart

TRUE FOODS FOR "TRUE LIFE"

TRUE FOOD JOURNAL

Day	Time	Morning	Afternoon	Evening
1				
2				
3				
4				
5				
6				
7				

Side Notes:

Date:

Mood:

Morning = Breakfast   Afternoon = Lunch   Evening = Dinner

Equational Poetry

Everyday Eating For "SELF" Chart

TRUE FOODS FOR "TRUE LIFE"

TRUE FOOD JOURNAL

Day	Time	Morning	Afternoon	Evening
1				
2				
3				
4				
5				
6				
7				

Side Notes:

Date:

Mood:

Morning = Breakfast   Afternoon = Lunch   Evening = Dinner

Equational Poetry

Everyday Eating For "SELF" Chart

TRUE FOODS FOR "TRUE LIFE"

TRUE FOOD JOURNAL

Day	Time	Morning	Afternoon	Evening
1				
2				
3				
4				
5				
6				
7				

Side Notes:

Date:

Mood:

Morning = Breakfast   Afternoon = Lunch   Evening = Dinner

Equational Poetry

Everyday Eating For "SELF" Chart

TRUE FOODS FOR "TRUE LIFE"

TRUE FOOD JOURNAL

Day	Time	Morning	Afternoon	Evening
1				
2				
3				
4				
5				
6				
7				

Side Notes:

Date:

Mood:

Morning = Breakfast   Afternoon = Lunch   Evening = Dinner

Equational Poetry

Everyday Eating For "SELF" Chart

TRUE FOODS FOR "TRUE LIFE"

TRUE FOOD JOURNAL

Day	Time	Morning	Afternoon	Evening
1				
2				
3				
4				
5				
6				
7				

Side Notes:

Date:

Mood:

Morning = Breakfast   Afternoon = Lunch   Evening = Dinner

3

Equational Poetry

Everyday Eating For "SELF" Chart

TRUE FOODS FOR "TRUE LIFE"

TRUE FOOD JOURNAL

Day	Time	Morning	Afternoon	Evening
1				
2				
3				
4				
5				
6				
7				

Side Notes:

Date:

Mood:

Morning = Breakfast   Afternoon = Lunch   Evening = Dinner

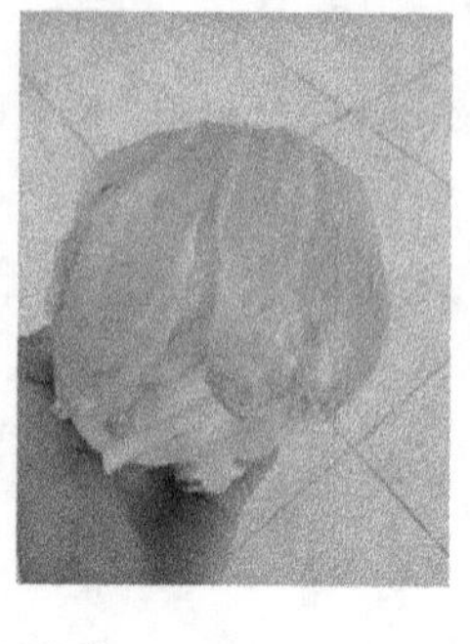

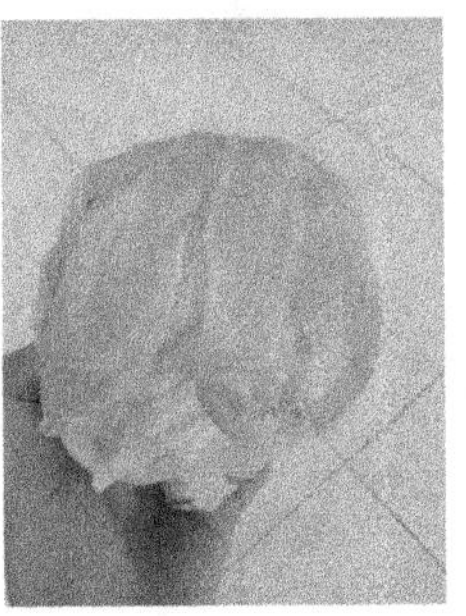

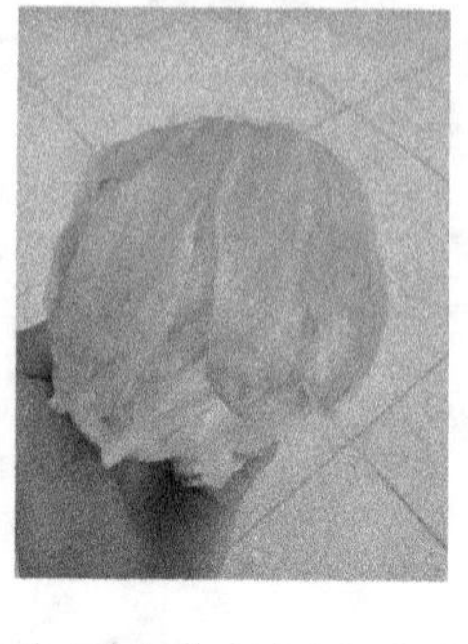

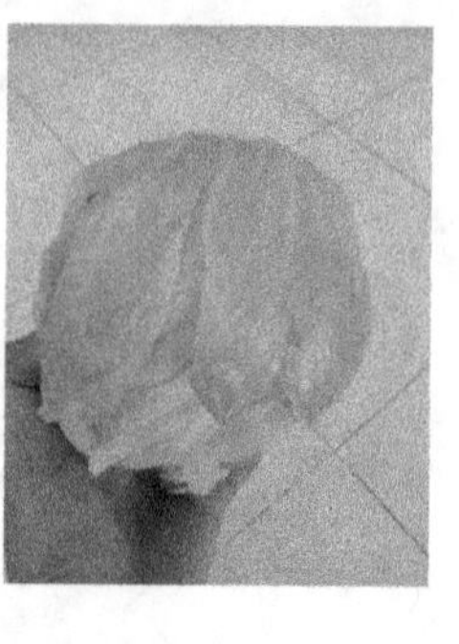

Equational Poetry

Everyday Eating For "SELF" Chart

TRUE FOODS FOR "TRUE LIFE"

TRUE FOOD JOURNAL

Day	Time	Morning	Afternoon	Evening
1				
2				
3				
4				
5				
6				
7				

Side Notes:

Date:

Mood:

Morning = Breakfast   Afternoon = Lunch   Evening = Dinner

Equational Poetry

Everyday Eating For "SELF" Chart

TRUE FOODS FOR "TRUE LIFE"

TRUE FOOD JOURNAL

Day	Time	Morning	Afternoon	Evening
1				
2				
3				
4				
5				
6				
7				

Side Notes:

Date:

Mood:

Morning = Breakfast   Afternoon = Lunch   Evening = Dinner

Equational Poetry

Everyday Eating For "SELF" Chart

TRUE FOODS FOR "TRUE LIFE"

TRUE FOOD JOURNAL

Day	Time	Morning	Afternoon	Evening
1				
2				
3				
4				
5				
6				
7				

Side Notes:

Date:

Mood:

Morning = Breakfast   Afternoon = Lunch   Evening = Dinner

Equational Poetry

Everyday Eating For "SELF" Chart

TRUE FOODS FOR "TRUE LIFE"

TRUE FOOD JOURNAL

Day	Time	Morning	Afternoon	Evening
1				
2				
3				
4				
5				
6				
7				

Side Notes:

Date:

Mood:

Morning = Breakfast   Afternoon = Lunch   Evening = Dinner

Equational Poetry

Everyday Eating For "SELF" Chart

TRUE FOODS FOR "TRUE LIFE"

TRUE FOOD JOURNAL

Day	Time	Morning	Afternoon	Evening
1				
2				
3				
4				
5				
6				
7				

Side Notes:

Date:

Mood:

Morning = Breakfast   Afternoon = Lunch   Evening = Dinner

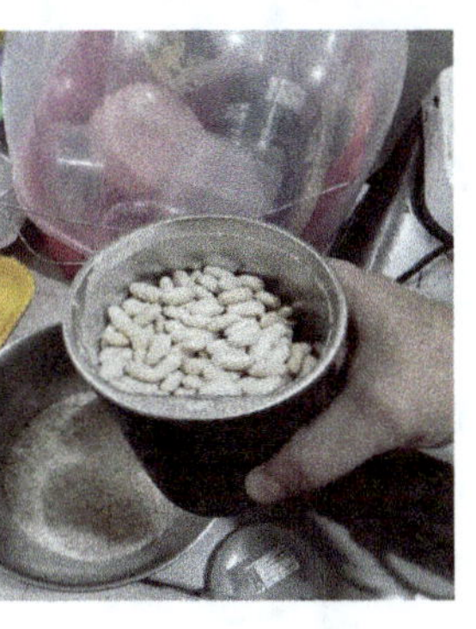

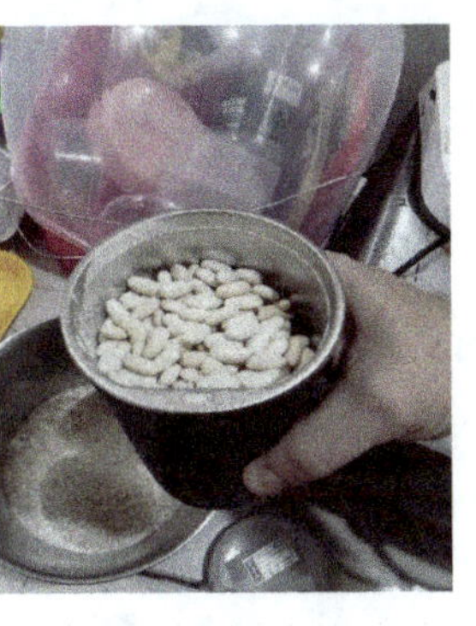

Equational Poetry

Everyday Eating For "SELF" Chart

TRUE FOODS FOR "TRUE LIFE"

TRUE FOOD JOURNAL

Day	Time	Morning	Afternoon	Evening
1				
2				
3				
4				
5				
6				
7				

Side Notes:

Date:

Mood:

Morning = Breakfast   Afternoon = Lunch   Evening = Dinner

3

Equational Poetry

Everyday Eating For "SELF" Chart

TRUE FOODS FOR "TRUE LIFE"

TRUE FOOD JOURNAL

Day	Time	Morning	Afternoon	Evening
1				
2				
3				
4				
5				
6				
7				

Side Notes:

Date:

Mood:

Morning = Breakfast   Afternoon = Lunch   Evening = Dinner

Equational Poetry

Everyday Eating For "SELF" Chart

TRUE FOODS FOR "TRUE LIFE"

TRUE FOOD JOURNAL

Day	Time	Morning	Afternoon	Evening
1				
2				
3				
4				
5				
6				
7				

Side Notes:

Date:

Mood:

Morning = Breakfast   Afternoon = Lunch   Evening = Dinner

Equational Poetry

Everyday Eating For "SELF" Chart

TRUE FOODS FOR "TRUE LIFE"

TRUE FOOD JOURNAL

Day	Time	Morning	Afternoon	Evening
1				
2				
3				
4				
5				
6				
7				

Side Notes:

Date:

Mood:

Morning = Breakfast   Afternoon = Lunch   Evening = Dinner

Equational Poetry

Everyday Eating For "SELF" Chart

TRUE FOODS FOR "TRUE LIFE"

TRUE FOOD JOURNAL

Day	Time	Morning	Afternoon	Evening
1				
2				
3				
4				
5				
6				
7				

Side Notes:

Date:

Mood:

Morning = Breakfast   Afternoon = Lunch   Evening = Dinner

Equational Poetry

Everyday Eating For "SELF" Chart

TRUE FOODS FOR "TRUE LIFE"

TRUE FOOD JOURNAL

Day	Time	Morning	Afternoon	Evening
1				
2				
3				
4				
5				
6				
7				

Side Notes:

Date:

Mood:

Morning = Breakfast   Afternoon = Lunch   Evening = Dinner

Vegan Pizza Pancakes.

Vegan Pizza Pancakes.

Vegan Pizza Pancakes.

Vegan Pizza Pancakes.

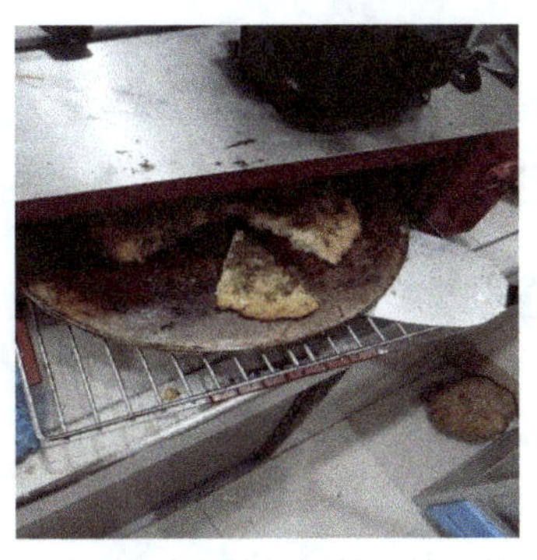

Vegan Pizza
Pancakes.

Vegan Pizza Pancakes.

Vegan Pizza Pancakes.

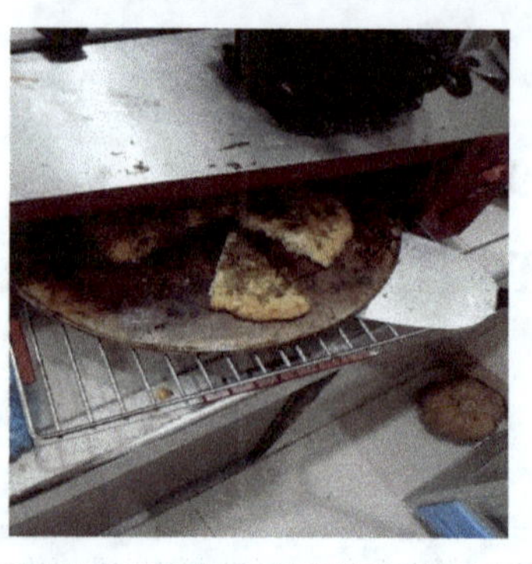

Equational Poetry

Everyday Eating For "SELF" Chart

TRUE FOODS FOR "TRUE LIFE"

TRUE FOOD JOURNAL

Day	Time	Morning	Afternoon	Evening
1				
2				
3				
4				
5				
6				
7				

Side Notes:

Date:

Mood:

Morning = Breakfast   Afternoon = Lunch   Evening = Dinner

"True" Foods
Banana

Our "True Senses" fade away and our chemical controlled "Slave Senses" takeover.

The Ultimate Vegan Diet is explained in Eating For "SELF."

"True" Foods
combinations can
complete the meal.

Protein is important, but don't eat too much because it can be dangerous?

The main book in The Health,
Diet & Recipe's Adventure
Book Series.

THE BELL CLOCK
Wholistic Health
Nowhere To Go
But Down:
The Quantum
Blue Skies
Out of The Domestic Marine (TM)
Series, Book 4

Equational Poetry
True Foods
Journal:
Eating For "SELF"

The Health, Diet, and Recipe's Adventure Book Series Tandem Writing paperback color graphic interior 213 Journal ruled blank pages personal writing food journal.

RICHARD JON HASSEY: AUTHOR of The Domestic marine ™ and Inventor of Tandem Book Writing and Inventor of The Television Commercial Silencer Electrical Wall Outlet Receptacle Tap (U.S. Patent No. 10,249,996) and led the Silencer Project, BOOK III of The Domestic marine ™ Tandem Book Writing and Equational and Engendered Poetry Series, with Parallel Writing.

Nelfa is the owner of NCRS Publishing and fantastic chef of Kakanin Plus (kakaninplus.com) consignment Real Filipino food, faithful mother of 4 children and my beautiful wife.

Equational Poetry
True Foods Journal:
Eating For "SELF"

"Equational Poetry" will examine your assessment charts and scores and their meanings, and determine if you are ready for the journey and adventure back to "True Life." Just visit:

https://www.equationalpoetryjournal.com

End Notes: